THE PRESIDENCY OF

George WASHINGTON

INSPIRING A YOUNG NATION

BY DANIELLE SMITH-LLERA

CONTENT CONSULTANT
RICHARD DOUGHERTY
PROFESSOR, DEPARTMENT OF POLITICS
UNIVERSITY OF DALLAS

COMPASS POINT BOOKS
a capstone imprint

Compass Point Books are published by Capstone,
1710 Roe Crest Drive, North Mankato, Minnesota 56003
www.capstonepub.com

Editorial Credits
Melissa York, editor; Becky Daum, designer; Maggie Villaume, production
specialist; Catherine Neitge and Ashlee Suker, consulting editor and designer

Photo Credits
Art Resource, N.Y.: The Metropolitan Museum of Art, 38; Corbis: 25, 42, 57
(top), Bettmann, 17, 37, 55; Library of Congress: 5, 6, 22, 30, 35, 51, 52, 59,
Marian Carson Collection, 21; National Archives and Records Administration,
11, 19, 57 (bottom), 58; North Wind Picture Archives, 12, 15, 29, 33, 41,
45, 47; Red Line Editorial, 49; Shutterstock Images, 27, 54; SuperStock:
Buyenlarge, cover
Art Elements: Shutterstock Images

Library of Congress Cataloging-in-Publication Data
Smith-Llera, Danielle, 1971–
  The presidency of George Washington: inspiring a young nation / by Danielle
Smith-Llera.
      pages cm.—(Greatest U.S. presidents)
  Includes bibliographical references and index.
  ISBN 978-0-7565-4928-2 (library binding)
  ISBN 978-0-7565-4936-7 (paperback)
  ISBN 978-0-7565-4944-2 (ebook PDF)
1. Washington, George, 1732–1799—Juvenile literature. 2. Presidents—
United States—Biography—Juvenile literature. 3. United States—Politics and
government—1789–1797—Juvenile literature. I. Title.
  E312.66.S66 2015
  973.4ʾ1092—dc23 [B]   2014006946

Printed in Canada.
032014   008086FRF14

TABLE OF CONTENTS

Chapter One

Becoming
PRESIDENT

Americans lined roads in towns and cities from Virginia to New York City, waiting for a glimpse of one man traveling north. They cheered, wept, and threw flowers as George Washington passed, traveling to his inauguration as the first president of the United States.

Crowds had cheered Washington along this same route years earlier when he was commander of the Continental army during the Revolutionary War (1775–1783). Taller than most men of his time at 6 feet 3 inches (190 centimeters), he had

George Washington was an American war hero before
he became the country's first president.

been a beloved military leader in his dark blue wool uniform coat sitting astride his white horse. Soldiers had sailed with him across the icy Delaware River at night for a victorious surprise attack on the British. Officers stood by him when the British were winning. Many became dear friends with whom he exchanged letters for a lifetime. For most Americans, Washington was a hero. He was unanimously elected president by the Electoral College. First he had represented the Revolution. Now he was going to represent the new government.

The people of Trenton, New Jersey, lined the street to watch Washington go by to his inauguration.

But while Washington waved to the gathered people in April 1789, anxiety gripped him. Before he set out he wrote that he felt similar to a person traveling to the "place of his execution." He worried that the people were expecting too much from one man. Along the road he glimpsed the eager faces of men who had fought for him as soldiers. He had led these men in war with confidence because the goal was relatively simple— freedom from the oppressive British government that taxed them outrageously. But now fulfilling their dreams for a new kind of government was complicated and full of risk.

Washington knew he faced an "ocean of difficulties" as president. He was inheriting a nation that had suffered in the six years since it won its freedom from Great Britain. Disillusioned Americans had seen clearly that the Articles of Confederation, in effect since 1781, did not produce a strong, unified country. Under the Articles each state government had made its own decisions about how the state would run. The federal government had consisted of only Congress, the legislative branch. The government was poor because it could not force states to send taxes to Congress. It was unable to pay soldiers to protect the nation. It could not sign trade agreements with foreign countries because each state had to approve a treaty separately.

Washington recognized the 13 states were a weak union barely holding together. He and other leaders of the time believed the nation needed a new kind of government, a republic in which power rested with the people. Thus this new republic needed a leader who was not a king. State leaders gathered at the Philadelphia Convention in 1787 and crafted a new Constitution. The document declared that the United

BRANCHES OF GOVERNMENT ESTABLISHED BY THE U.S. CONSTITUTION

Legislative Makes laws	Executive Carries out laws	Judicial Settles disputes over laws
Congress (House of Representatives and Senate)	President Vice President	Supreme Court Lower Federal Courts

States would have a strong central government, headed by an elected president.

As Washington traveled past the adoring crowds, he knew many citizens were wary of a powerful president who might abuse his power over the states. The powerlessness these Americans had felt at the hands of the British monarchy was still a fresh memory. Some states had only reluctantly ratified the Constitution after much negotiation. Two states had still not ratified it at the time of Washington's inauguration.

Washington's supporters cried out "Long live George Washington" as his carriage rolled past. Europe celebrated its kings in this fashion. In order to win the trust of his citizens, Washington would have to prove he did not wish to rule as a king. He bowed modestly and tipped his hat to his admirers. Washington had willingly resigned his position as commander in chief in 1783, after the Revolutionary War, and returned to his life in the country. He gave up power when he had it in hand, unlike many military leaders in history who turned into military dictators.

As Washington approached New York, he hoped to avoid more ceremony. Instead, cannons boomed as a boat carried him across the harbor, serenaded by musicians on other boats. Washington disembarked and found carpeted steps and a carriage waiting to take him to his lodging in the nation's temporary capital. He surprised everyone by choosing to walk instead.

Washington knew he was setting an example in everything he did. He believed it was important for the American president to be humble. Instead of being called "His Excellency," he chose the simpler address "Mr. President." He announced he did not wish to receive a salary for serving in office (though Congress paid him one anyway). But he also expected an American president to lead with dignity and authority. He usually appeared in public with a sword at his side. He also refused to shake hands because he believed it was not an appropriate gesture for a president.

He stood on the balcony of the white-columned Federal Hall in New York City on April 30, 1789, with his hand resting on a Bible to take the presidential oath. An awed crowd watched from below. He swore to "faithfully execute the office of President of the United States" and to "preserve, protect, and defend the Constitution of the United States." He proved his faith to the new, independent nation by wearing a plain brown suit made in the United States, not imported from Great Britain. His silver buttons were decorated with eagles, a nod to the bald eagle Congress had chosen as a symbol of the new country.

Yet Washington trembled when he stood solemnly before Congress to deliver his inaugural address inside Federal Hall. A senator noticed that Washington appeared more upset than he ever had during the war, even when guns were pointed at him. Finally Washington spoke in a voice so low that the listeners had to lean forward. The 57-year-old president spoke of doubting his own worthiness and skill but also of hearing

Washington's handwritten copy of his first inaugural address

the "voice of my Country" calling. He spoke of establishing the

new government as an "experiment entrusted to the hands of

the American people." He acknowledged that it could fail. But

he trusted that members of Congress, with their patriotism and

good character, would work with him toward the "preservation

of the sacred fire of liberty."

A LIFE
OF SERVICE

An elegant dancer, fine horseman, innovative farmer, loyal friend, and the United States' first president, George Washington was born February 22, 1732, on a simple farm in Westmoreland County, Virginia. He was 11 when his father died. Gifted in numbers, he trained himself as a surveyor and set out to map the western wilderness.

Washington joined the Virginia militia in 1752. Tensions were increasing between the British and the French in the Ohio River region, and the colonial militias fought alongside the British army. Eventually rising to colonel, Washington helped the British win several key battles in the French and Indian War (1754–1763). By the time he resigned in 1758 to take office in the Virginia legislature, the House of Burgesses, he was commander of all Virginia troops.

Washington married wealthy widow Martha Custis in 1759. Martha's two children, John "Jacky" and Martha "Patsy" Custis, were

4 and 2, and Washington raised them as his own. The Washingtons settled into life running the farms of George's estate, Mount Vernon, which he had inherited from his half-brother in 1752. George was devastated when Patsy died at age 17 following an epileptic seizure. When Jacky died in 1781, George adopted the youngest two of Jacky's four children and cared for them as a father.

In 1774 Washington joined other colonial leaders at the First Continental Congress to discuss their problems with Great Britain. War broke out in April 1775, and the Second Continental Congress appointed Washington commander of the Continental army on June 15. The colonists suffered many defeats. But the turning point came December 25, 1776, when Washington led an attack across the Delaware River that surprised British troops at Trenton. More victories followed, and with the help of the French and Washington's strategy, Americans won their independence in 1783. There was little question of Americans choosing anyone else for their first president.

Washington served two four-year terms as president. He left office in March 1797 and retired to Mount Vernon. He went for a horseback ride in the snow December 12, 1799, and woke up the next morning with a severe sore throat. He lost strength rapidly and the doctors' treatments, including bloodletting, were not helpful. He died December 14, 1799, at age 67.

Chapter Two

Building
THE UNION

As a young man working as a surveyor, George Washington learned how to map wilderness areas. In the same way, setting up the new government was, in his words, like walking on "untrodden ground." The Constitution was his surveying tool for mapping out the new republic. Having helped craft it, he was well aware that it left many unanswered questions about how to proceed. He would need help shaping the new government.

Washington did not believe in leading alone. As a military commander, he had wrestled with the question of how his

Washington surveyed land purchases in the western frontier of Virginia in the 1750s.

scrappy army could defeat the large, well-trained British one.
He regularly called meetings with his generals. He listened
quietly to differing points of view. Later, in private, he would
carefully consider what he had heard and make his decision.

As he had on the battlefield, Washington assembled a group
of advisers to serve with him in the executive office. Because
he was older—a symbol of the country's revolution and early
struggles—he chose four younger men who represented the
young nation's future. Washington also hoped these important

advisers, whom he called secretaries, would act as a unifying force. They would represent various regions of the country and different ideas about how the government should run. This group of advisers has come to be known as the Cabinet. Though not described in the Constitution, the Cabinet has been part of the executive branch ever since.

Washington, a southerner, appointed two northerners along with two southerners to his Cabinet. Alexander Hamilton, secretary of the treasury, was a banker from New York. Henry Knox, secretary of war, was a businessman from Massachusetts. Edmund Randolph, the attorney general, was a lawyer from Virginia. And Thomas Jefferson, secretary of state, was a Virginia planter.

With these appointments Washington hoped to please New York and Virginia. These two large, wealthy states were among the ones that most distrusted a strong federal government. Each had reluctantly ratified the Constitution while recommending an addition to the document. They wanted the Constitution to list people's rights that the government could never take away. Jefferson argued that this protection from a powerful government was necessary. Americans had fought a long war to win rights not protected by the British king.

Washington with his Cabinet (from left), Henry Knox, Alexander Hamilton, Thomas Jefferson, and Edmund Randolph

Washington wanted to assure Americans he was not a king in disguise. He affirmed he was a public servant eager to "know the will of my masters." Having advocated for the "rights of freemen" in his inaugural address, he welcomed the passage of the Bill of Rights. The 10 amendments to the Constitution extended greater protection to the people for a variety of rights, among them freedom of speech and free exercise of religion.

Yet the Bill of Rights failed to reassure the new president's strongest critics, including Jefferson. These critics feared the federal government still had too much power. Meanwhile,

Washington worried as two opposing groups—the Federalists and the Anti-Federalists—voiced increasingly stronger opinions about how the republic should function. Washington would struggle throughout his presidency with balancing these two new political parties.

Federalists believed that as long as a strong federal government kept its power spread among many people, it would not abuse its authority over people and their states. In contrast, the Anti-Federalists believed a federal government headed by a powerful president would rob the states and ultimately the people of the right to make independent decisions.

Washington believed the structure of the government prevented the Anti-Federalists' worst fears from coming true. With a system of checks and balances, Washington believed that he, the head of the executive branch, was only one part of a larger system. He believed Congress was the true voice of the people, not him.

Washington did not build the government around the presidency, like a king would have. Through words and actions, he demonstrated his belief that the other branches of government supported the legislative one. He felt it was his duty as president both to ensure that laws created in the legislative

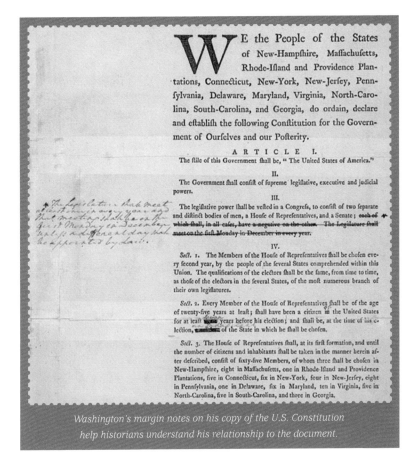

Washington's margin notes on his copy of the U.S. Constitution help historians understand his relationship to the document.

branch did not violate the Constitution and to enforce the laws.

To assist him in evaluating and carrying out the laws, he focused

on strengthening the third branch of government, the judiciary.

Washington signed the Judiciary Act of 1789, which created

a network of courts throughout the country. The Supreme

Court, the highest federal court, would have a chief justice and

five associate justices. It would decide whether rulings in lower

courts violated the Constitution. Washington considered an

organized judiciary vital to the new nation. As he told Edmund

Randolph in a letter asking him to accept the newly created position of attorney general, "The due administration of justice is the firmest pillar of government."

But debates over the proper power of the federal courts again divided the public. Federalists were confident that the separation of powers prevented the government from abusing the people. Anti-Federalists were not comforted by federal power being spread more evenly among the three branches of government. They feared that the Supreme Court's power to reverse decisions made in state courthouses would undermine the interests of the states. The debate over the division of power among the branches of the federal government and between the national and state level would continue.

Washington knew that bringing order to the new nation also meant organizing its finances. In 1783 in Newburgh, New York, Washington had seen how quickly money troubles could spark a revolution. Angry Continental army soldiers had gathered, outraged because Congress had not paid them in weeks. They were on the brink of revolt. Some military members advised Washington, their commander at the time, to take on the powers of a dictator and force Congress to pay the troops.

Instead, Washington stepped before the restless group and humbly urged the men not to take up arms.

Washington now stood before the new but poor nation as its president. Years after the war's end, thousands of veterans had not received their full salaries. States had been functioning like small, independent countries and had difficulty conducting business with each other. Banks printed their own currencies.

As he had demonstrated on the battlefield, Washington was skilled at choosing the right person for a task. He trusted

Rhode Island currency from 1786

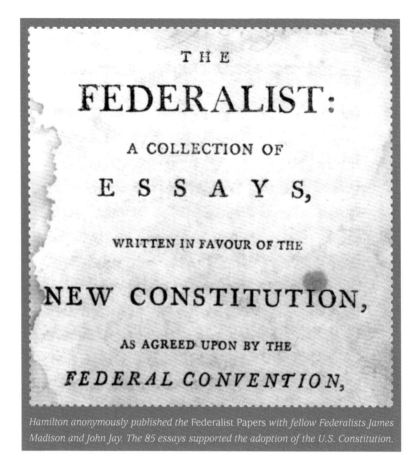

THE

FEDERALIST:

A COLLECTION OF

E S S A Y S,

WRITTEN IN FAVOUR OF THE

NEW CONSTITUTION,

AS AGREED UPON BY THE

FEDERAL CONVENTION,

Hamilton anonymously published the Federalist Papers *with fellow Federalists James Madison and John Jay. The 85 essays supported the adoption of the U.S. Constitution.*

Secretary of the Treasury Alexander Hamilton to find a solution to the financial crisis. Hamilton had spent years studying the economic systems of European countries. Having helped establish the Bank of New York before joining the Cabinet, he leapt at the challenge to find a way to put the nation's finances in order.

Washington remained in the background as his secretary persuaded Congress. Hamilton believed the country, with its vast natural resources, could become a center of manufacturing and international trade. Yet the federal government and individual states had owed foreign powers tens of millions of dollars ever since the Revolutionary War. As a result, Hamilton argued, foreign countries were suspicious of the United States and reluctant to set up businesses there. Hamilton believed that without better relationships with foreign countries, the nation would have few trading partners. With no trade, the nation would remain poor and weak.

Debate flared when Hamilton offered Congress a solution. He called his solution "assumption" because the federal government would assume all the states' debts. Northerners, who were mostly Federalists, welcomed the federal government's involvement in the states' affairs. They were especially enthusiastic because they had not paid off their war debts. Southerners, who were mostly Anti-Federalists, protested that the federal government was grabbing too much power. Jefferson led this accusation. Moreover, the southern states had already repaid most of their debts.

Washington welcomed discussion but worried that the debates over the debts had turned bitter. He was concerned that this debate made the divide between North and South "more strongly marked than could have been wished." Hamilton finally offered the Anti-Federalist southerners a tempting compromise. If they voted for his financial plan, then northerners would vote to build the permanent federal capital in the South. In the end the Assumption Act and Residence Act both passed in 1790. Washington chose land between Virginia and Maryland for what would become Washington, D.C.

Washington had to publicly take a position on Hamilton's financial plan. Hamilton had proposed and then guided a bill through Congress establishing the Bank of the United States and a single national currency. He had also proposed a tax on alcohol to raise more funds for the federal government. The bank bill now sat on Washington's desk, awaiting his signature to become law.

Washington sought his Cabinet's advice on whether he should sign the bill. Jefferson argued that the power to create a national bank was not specifically allowed by the Constitution. Hamilton responded that the Constitution needed to be flexible for the nation to survive. The fact that Congress had approved the bill reassured Washington greatly. He did not typically stand against Congress. Washington would only exercise the president's veto power over Congress's proposed bills twice in his eight years in office. Washington signed the Bank Act of

DEBATE OVER THE NEW CAPITAL

The Residence Act granted Washington permission to select the site of the new capital along the banks of the Potomac River. He selected a hilly area of forests and swamps not far from Mount Vernon. While three commissioners oversaw the project, Washington was eager for the future city to reflect his vision for the new nation. Washington entrusted Pierre Charles L'Enfant to sketch the layout of the streets. However, Jefferson—a lover of architecture—had already sketched out his own vision of the new capital.

Debate erupted over the capital's design. Washington's belief in a strong federal government favored L'Enfant's grand design for a city of broad avenues, elaborate buildings, and dramatic views. Jefferson believed the federal government should be small and limited in power. He envisioned modest public buildings. Ultimately the commissioners followed L'Enfant's plan.

Washington laid the cornerstone of the U.S. Capitol building September 18, 1793. L'Enfant's design still influences the layout of the current city. While it resembles old European cities in many ways, its features also reflect the vision of a new republic. The Capitol building, home of Congress, dominates the city from its hill. This makes the Capitol the most important building in the city, rather than the president's home. And stretching out from the Capitol is a wide lawn, called the Mall, which invites all people to gather as equals.

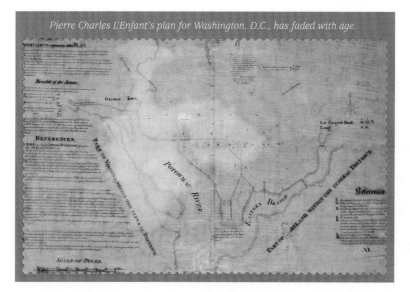

Pierre Charles L'Enfant's plan for Washington, D.C., has faded with age.

1791 into law with confidence, proclaiming, "Our public credit is restored, our resources are increasing."

The battle over Hamilton's financial plan was a symptom of the fierce rivalry between the two brilliant secretaries. Hamilton's Federalist ideas and his ability to persuade were balanced by Jefferson's Anti-Federalist ideas and equal charisma. Hamilton believed so firmly in strong government that he once argued American presidents should serve for life as monarchs did. Jefferson, meanwhile, believed that "men are capable of governing themselves without a master." Washington tried to stay neutral and provide a balance between the two viewpoints.

But clashes continued between Hamilton's Federalist Party and Jefferson's Anti-Federalist Party, renamed the Republican Party, and, later still, the Democratic-Republican Party. At the end of his first term, Washington yearned to retire to a quiet life at Mount Vernon. He even started planning for a farewell address. He was exhausted trying to make peace within his Cabinet and,

IT'S A FACT

Though Washington selected the site for the president's residence, he never lived in it. President John Adams was the first president to live there, moving to the unfinished White House in 1800.

Built in 1735, the original house at Mount Vernon was smaller. Washington gradually enlarged it to 21 rooms.

ultimately, within the nation. Yet even Jefferson believed that the new nation was not mature enough to flourish without its founding father.

The nation was not ready to let him go, and Washington was re-elected unanimously. Washington was growing old and tired, but he would do what he believed to be his duty. At his request his second inauguration was a much simpler affair. The president rode to Congress Hall in Philadelphia in his carriage by himself. But crowds gathered to cheer for Washington as he left his oath-taking ceremony. The people were eager for him to continue leading them.

Chapter Three

Staying
THE COURSE

As violent change swept through Europe, George Washington worried about his fragile new government. French revolutionaries rebelled against their monarchy, beheading King Louis XVI at the guillotine in January 1793. The new French government soon declared war on its longtime enemy Great Britain and then on other European countries. France wanted to spread a general revolution against monarchy while also extending its borders.

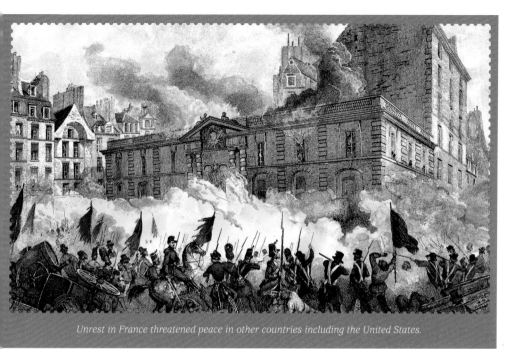

Unrest in France threatened peace in other countries including the United States.

The war across the ocean created war within Washington's Cabinet. Alexander Hamilton and Thomas Jefferson clashed more fiercely than ever. Hamilton had long admired how Great Britain managed its government. He also believed the United States' health depended on open trade and peaceful relations with other countries. He urged the president not to join France in its war against Great Britain or any other foreign war.

Jefferson believed Americans shared a deep connection with the French people because they had also revolted against a monarchy. Furthermore, because the French had helped Americans win the Revolutionary War, Jefferson passionately argued it was the United States' moral duty to help them.

Washington desperately wanted to avoid drawing his young nation into war. He believed the new country needed stability in order to thrive, and it had no army or navy to speak of. The United States had signed an alliance with France during the Revolutionary War. But Washington was wary of its new, violent government. Ongoing problems with Great Britain since the Revolutionary War, however, discouraged him from wanting to help his old enemy. His solution was to take neither France's nor

Arguments broke out within the Cabinet and Congress and throughout the country over whether Washington had too much power.

Great Britain's side. He announced a Neutrality Proclamation in April 1793, which declared the United States would remain "friendly and impartial" to countries at war. The Cabinet publicly supported Washington's announcement. But Jefferson concluded that Washington had acted like a monarch by issuing the proclamation without the advice of Congress, which some argued had absolute authority over foreign affairs.

Washington had thought the Atlantic Ocean would keep the turmoil in France from reaching American shores. But when Edmond-Charles Genet, the new French representative to the United States, sailed into Charleston, South Carolina, in April 1793, he brought the explosive ideas of the French Revolution with him. Washington received reports that the charming Genet was traveling the country. The Frenchman spoke to gatherings of Americans, arguing that not supporting France meant not supporting freedom. Genet hoped that if he could persuade a majority of Americans to fight alongside France, then Washington would feel pressure to give up neutrality. The crowds waiting for Genet grew larger and more enthusiastic. In some areas those who did not support France and its revolution—mostly the Federalists—were even threatened with violence.

Democratic-Republican Societies formed in the 1790s, beginning in Philadelphia and spreading out across the country. The societies worried an aristocracy might form in the United States, so members encouraged the people in their communities to keep participating in democracy. They were in favor of the French Revolution and also supported free speech and freedom of the press. They wanted to prevent the federal government from gaining too much power.

Genet was delighted to find that Americans embraced the spirit of rebellion. From Vermont to South Carolina, citizens were forming what they called Democratic-Republican Societies. Genet encouraged these gatherings, where members celebrated the French Revolution's triumph over the monarchy and argued against favorable American relations with Great Britain.

In Philadelphia, Washington could hear Democratic-Republican crowds shouting their support for France. Washington was disturbed to learn that Genet was outfitting a warship to attack British vessels. Not only was the ship docked in the capital, Philadelphia, but Genet was inviting Americans to serve as its crew. Genet appeared to be single-handedly trying to push the United States into war with Great Britain.

Washington worried that Genet's words and actions could "shake the government to its foundation." He consulted with

Edmond-Charles Genet's visit to the U.S. and the events that followed are known in history as the Citizen Genet Affair.

his Cabinet on a plan of action. Jefferson argued for gentle treatment of the French representative. Hamilton clamored for him to be sent speedily back to France. Their debates about Genet's behavior were fierce. At times when his secretaries could find no compromise, Washington sent them off to write their opinions privately. As always, he carefully weighed their advice before taking action.

Washington made a decision he hoped would keep the peace between the United States and France. He chose Jefferson for the delicate task of writing to the French government, requesting Genet be recalled to France. But Genet would not be a problem for much longer. Soon Washington was relieved to hear that the French government had changed hands, and Genet was now considered an enemy of the new leaders. Washington allowed Genet to live in the United States, but Federalists savored his loss of power over Americans.

Washington's Cabinet did not survive these controversies intact, however. In a July 31, 1793, letter to Washington, Jefferson announced his retirement from the Cabinet. Despite their disagreements, Washington would miss Jefferson in his inner circle. He rode alone to Jefferson's country house to urge him to reconsider. But Jefferson chose to retire to his Virginia plantation. Without Jefferson's strong views and brilliance to counter Hamilton's, Washington worried about balance in his Cabinet.

SLAVERY IN THE NEW NATION

Growing up in Virginia, where nearly half the population was enslaved, Washington believed owning slaves was normal. Slavery was practiced throughout all the American colonies. At age 11, Washington inherited his father's farm and the 10 slaves he had owned. By the end of his life, Washington owned a large plantation with many slaves.

Washington wrestled with the morality of enslaving people, though he never publicly supported ending the practice. Shortly before becoming president, he wrote, "There is not a man living who wishes more sincerely than I do, to see a plan adopted for the abolition" of slavery. Yet he was cautious and favored only gradually freeing slaves. His faith ultimately rested in Congress and its ability to make new laws that would one day end slavery.

At the end of his life, Washington put his beliefs into action. His will stated that all his slaves—more than 300—were to be freed at the time of his wife Martha's death. Slavery continued to divide the country and would eventually lead to the bloody Civil War (1861–1865).

Accounts conflict and historians disagree about how Washington treated the enslaved people at Mount Vernon.

Chapter Four

War and
PEACE

George Washington had done all he could to avoid a war
overseas. Next he faced a violent conflict at home. Farmers near
the frontier in western Pennsylvania were frustrated with the
tax on alcohol. They grew grain and distilled it into whiskey,
which made their harvest easier to trade and transport. People
then traded the whiskey instead of using money. The federal
tax meant they now owed the government money each time
they turned grain into whiskey. Since 1791 disgruntled farmers
had harassed tax officials. They grumbled about wanting

Citizens tarred and feathered tax collectors in protest over the whiskey tax.

independence from the United States. Supporters of the federal government's laws were afraid to speak up.

Washington feared other rebellions could spark around the country. He was wary of the Democratic-Republican Societies and blamed them for stirring up the unrest in Pennsylvania. Once again Washington's Cabinet disagreed. Alexander Hamilton encouraged the president to use military force to end the rebellion. The Democratic-Republicans worried about the government raising an army against its own citizens.

A band of about 500 men burned the house of a tax inspector in July 1794. With order unraveling, Washington sent federal agents to Pennsylvania to reason with the farmers. Negotiations failed, and the agents told the president he would need to send soldiers. Washington declared he could not allow laws to be "trampled upon" without consequences.

The Constitution required the president to enforce laws passed by Congress.

Washington marched west in August. But by the time his army of 13,000 men arrived, the small group of rebels had scattered. Washington later wrote with satisfaction of ending the Whiskey Rebellion "without spilling a drop of blood."

What Democratic-Republicans feared most was a president backed by a powerful military force stripping states and people of their freedom. But their concern was unfounded. Washington sent his army home except for a small peacekeeping force. About 150 men were tried for treason but only two were convicted. Washington later pardoned them.

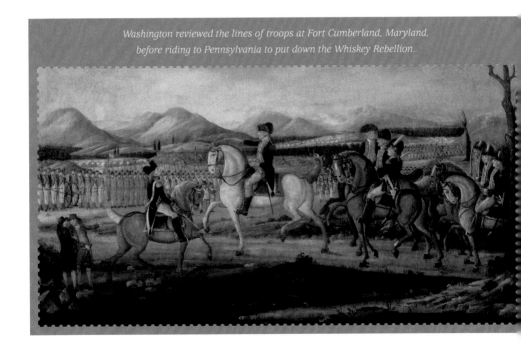

Washington reviewed the lines of troops at Fort Cumberland, Maryland, before riding to Pennsylvania to put down the Whiskey Rebellion.

While Washington was restoring order at home, he watched trouble unfolding on the Atlantic Ocean with an old enemy. Great Britain—still at war with France—ordered its ships to seize U.S. ships carrying certain French goods or delivering goods to France or its territories. Captured American sailors were forced to work for the British navy. Washington wondered how much longer the nation could remain neutral in the European war.

Americans had long resented the unfair way goods were traded between the countries. Great Britain benefited much more from trading with the United States. British goods, such as tea, cloth, and furniture, arrived at American ports in great supply. Americans bought these goods eagerly. Meanwhile, the British government made it nearly impossible for American goods such as tobacco and lumber to enter Great Britain. It also limited U.S. trade with the British West Indies, the tropical Caribbean islands that produced molasses, sugar, and cotton.

Washington had to face ongoing tension with the British in the forests of the American frontier as well. The British never left American soil entirely as they were supposed to according to the Treaty of Paris, which had formally ended the Revolutionary War in 1783. British soldiers occupied forts in the

PIRATE TROUBLE

Americans lost the protection of the British navy when they became independent. American ships then began suffering ruthless attacks by pirates supported by the Barbary powers, based in North Africa. Pirates seized ships, collected ransoms, and enslaved and killed hundreds of American hostages. The United States reluctantly agreed to buy protection for its ships by paying enormous amounts of money to the ruler of Algiers each year. Washington grew increasingly frustrated with the costly and unfair arrangement.

As attacks on American ships increased by both the British and pirates, Washington knew the country needed to build a formidable navy. In 1794 he signed a bill to pay for the construction of six warships mounted with cannons. The ships helped later presidents resolve problems with Algiers.

northern frontier and supported Native Americans in battles with American settlers.

Washington wondered how to keep the nation neutral as Great Britain continued to interfere in the new country's affairs. He first turned to his colleagues and Congress for their opinions. Both parties agreed that Great Britain's actions were outrageous. Yet the Federalists felt the United States could not afford to start a war with the world's most powerful navy. They believed that negotiating with the British could avoid an armed conflict. Jefferson's political party, however, still believed in the French cause and in taking a strong stand against monarchies such as

Great Britain's. It had no interest in making compromises with France's enemy.

A group of congressmen urged Washington to send a diplomat to Great Britain to discuss the two countries' issues. The president appointed Chief Justice of the United States John Jay, a devoted Federalist, to negotiate a new treaty with Great Britain. Meanwhile, to keep relations with France stable, the government also dispatched an envoy to France to shower praise on its government and citizens.

Washington told Jay to "cultivate peace with sincerity." And he also gave Jay clear demands. Jay was to refuse a treaty that

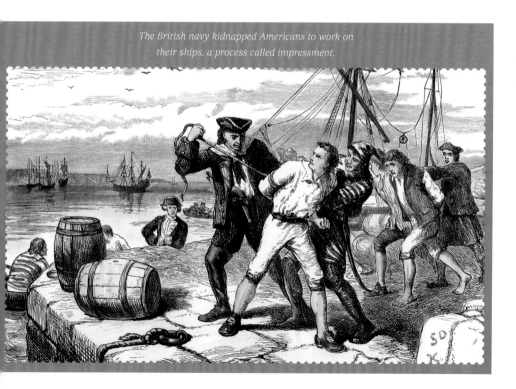

The British navy kidnapped Americans to work on their ships, a process called impressment.

would endanger the relationship between France and the United States. He also was to refuse a treaty that failed to open up the British West Indies to U.S. trade.

The final Jay Treaty, as it came to be called, was a compromise with the British that did not get everything Washington had hoped for. The British agreed to leave U.S. soil entirely, but not for two more years. Also, while Great Britain agreed to make the United States a special trading partner, it did so with serious restrictions. The treaty only allowed very small

John Jay later served as governor of New York and helped outlaw slavery in the state.

American ships to trade in the West Indies. American ships were forbidden from trading high-profit goods from the islands with other countries. The treaty even allowed the British to seize goods from American ships carrying cargo to France as long as Britain paid for what it took. The greatest disappointment was that the treaty did not forbid British ships from capturing American sailors at sea.

Washington took comfort in the fact that at least any treaty with Great Britain meant avoiding war. But he kept the treaty private for several months. Once Congress was back in session, Washington followed the Constitution's requirements and submitted the treaty to the Senate for review. Grateful to have the legislative body debate the unpopular treaty, he enclosed a note stating his reliance on the senators' advice to decide how to proceed. After more than a week of intense arguing, the Senate passed the Jay Treaty on June 24, 1795, by the minimum two-thirds vote.

When an unauthorized copy of the treaty appeared in newspapers, Americans could read all the details. Throughout the country Americans showed their outrage over a treaty that so favored the British. Mobs dragged the British flag through the streets and burned copies of the treaty. An audience in

New York City threw stones and drove Hamilton from a stage where he was attempting to give a speech.

Once the Senate approved the treaty, it sat on Washington's desk awaiting his signature to go into effect. The British would also have to sign it. Washington was not one to abandon his post. But for the first time in his presidency, he slipped off to Mount Vernon in the middle of a crisis, the unpopular treaty still unsigned. Along the way home, he questioned many he met about their reactions to the treaty. Washington deliberated whether to sign the treaty as he considered the potentially violent consequences of doing so. Ratifying the treaty would outrage the pro-French Democratic-Republicans and could start a war with France. Not ratifying the treaty would outrage the pro-British Federalists and could start a war with Great Britain. From his Virginia plantation home, Thomas Jefferson imagined that the crisis over the treaty meant the end of the Federalist Party. Meanwhile, British ships

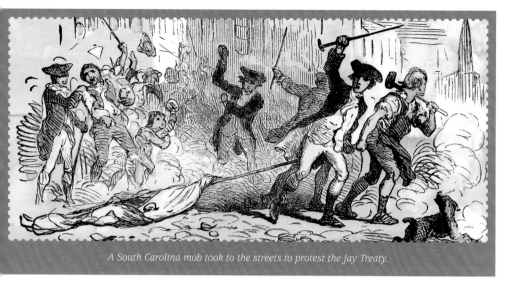
A South Carolina mob took to the streets to protest the Jay Treaty.

continued boldly seizing American ships loaded with grain on their way to France.

Finally Washington decided that war with Great Britain would be more disastrous than war with France. He signed the Jay Treaty in late 1795. Public protests against Washington and the treaty continued until 1796. French ships harassed American ones and even exchanged fire with them in later years. But Washington spared the United States a war with Great Britain so the young country could continue to mature and become self-reliant.

The tensions with other countries fueled a fight that had been brewing in American frontier forests for decades. Since the Revolutionary War, American settlers moving into western regions around modern-day Ohio had clashed violently with

Native Americans. The Native Americans were defending the lands where they had lived for centuries. They were fighting against settlers who had been seizing land from them by force. The Native Americans were armed with weapons supplied by British troops, who still occupied forts on American soil.

Washington struggled to find a way to end this war in the Northwest. Early in his presidency, he was determined to keep in mind "the great principles of Justice and humanity" when working with Native Americans. He had sent government officials bearing gifts to the American Indians in the frontier. Sometimes they would all sit together around fires to talk peacefully. At other times there were gunshots.

Despite signing treaties with tribes in the region, the U.S. government did nothing effective to stop Americans from settling farther and farther into American Indian territory. Displaced tribes attacked to push back the intruders. In response Washington resorted to force to protect his citizens. Twice he sent armies into the Northwest Territories and twice Native Americans armed by the British defeated the United States. In 1794 Washington sent Anthony Wayne, a well-known Revolutionary War general, to lead a well-trained army of 4,000 men against a group of 2,000 Native Americans from

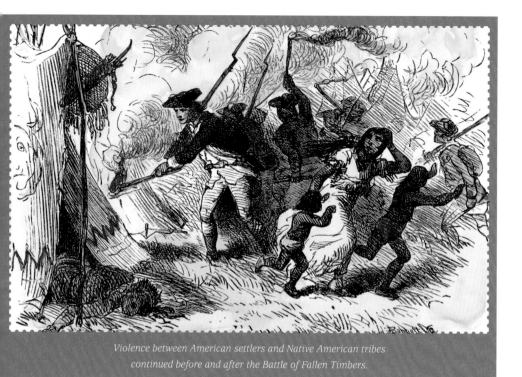
Violence between American settlers and Native American tribes continued before and after the Battle of Fallen Timbers.

a confederation of several tribes. Outnumbered, the Native Americans fled and were refused help from the British at a nearby fort. Great Britain had decided not to provoke the United States any further.

Tribes in the region felt defeated because they could no longer depend on British support. This Battle of Fallen Timbers effectively ended the Northwest Indian War, although isolated confrontations between tribe members and white settlers continued. In the Treaty of Greenville of 1795, the confederation of tribes surrendered large areas of the western territories to the United States. The U.S. victory over the tribes in the northwestern frontier finally pushed the British from American soil.

On the southwestern frontier, Americans confronted yet another European power. Near modern-day Florida and Georgia, Americans clashed with Native Americans armed by Spain. Meanwhile, the Jay Treaty made Spain fear for the safety of its colonies, surrounded as they were by the United States and British colonies. While the United States was growing in size and wealth, Spain was struggling to maintain its empire and alliances with other powers.

Spain was eager to improve relations with the United States. Washington saw an opportunity to expand American borders and increase the nation's wealth. He sent southern Federalist Thomas Pinckney, who asked Spain to settle the dispute over the border between the United States and Spanish colonies. Spain accepted that the U.S. border would extend all the way to the Mississippi River. Spain also promised to stop supporting Native American tribes fighting against American settlers.

Pinckney also insisted that Spain allow American ships to use the port in Spanish-held New Orleans, at the mouth of the Mississippi River. Spain begrudgingly agreed, and American goods from the Ohio River Valley and the U.S. interior could

Disputed with United Kingdom

Disputed with United Kingdom

New Hampshire

Vermont

Connecticut Western Reserve

Massachusetts

New York

Rhode Island

Connecticut

Pennsylvania

New Jersey

Northwest Territory

Delaware

Virginia

Maryland

France

Kentucky

Tennessee

North Carolina

South Carolina

State

Territory

Georgia

France

Spain

Spain

Disputed area

The United States and territories, 1796

now travel down the great river, out to sea, and on to Europe without being taxed by Spain.

Washington promptly sent the treaty along to Congress, where it was passed with great enthusiasm. Because of Washington's treaties with Spain and with Native American tribes, the frontier was safer for American settlement. As trade flowed more freely in the American western regions, the frontier became wealthier. Americans now felt more confident about moving westward. As Washington had wished, negotiations and treaties brought the peace that allowed the new nation to thrive.

Washington's
FAREWELL

George Washington quietly rode away from Philadelphia toward Mount Vernon on September 19, 1796. Back in the city, a newspaper headline announced, "President to Resign; Issues Solemn Warnings to Nation." News spread through the country, and then the world, that Washington was surrendering his position of power—willingly.

Most Americans were deeply moved by the news of Washington's decision not to seek a third term. While there was fear and uncertainty, there was also surprise and

After eight years in office, Washington was ready to retire to Mount Vernon.

admiration at his humble decision. Thirteen years earlier King George III refused to believe Washington's promise to resign as commander and return to his farm after winning the war against Great Britain. In fact he claimed Washington would be the "greatest man in the world" if he did. Now Washington wanted to set an example for any future presidents tempted to stay in office until death, like a king. Every president who followed him, except for Franklin Delano Roosevelt, served no longer than two elected terms. The Constitution was changed to make two terms the limit in 1951.

After years of service as commander, Constitution framer, and president, Washington felt the "increasing weight of years." At age 64, riding on horseback left him sore. His mouth ached from the false teeth he wore because he had lost most of his own. But most of all, the old war hero suffered from a battered reputation. He felt his mind was even more "worn away" than his body. Washington lamented that while the United States was "encompassed on all sides with avowed enemies and insidious friends," it was battles within its borders—within the government itself—that were tearing the nation apart.

Washington's retirement allowed him to spend more time with his wife and grandchildren.

Printed under the headline announcing his retirement was Washington's open letter to "Friends and Fellow-Citizens." In writing the 32-page document, he had consulted with colleagues Alexander Hamilton, John Jay, and James Madison, a Federalist and an author of the Bill of Rights. Washington wanted his message to the American people to be clear. His letter offers firm advice and strong warnings not only to Americans at the time, but to future generations.

Washington's Farewell Address reminded citizens that they had the power to keep their union together. He urged the American people to be loyal to their nation, not simply to the region where they lived. Perhaps considering the Whiskey Rebellion, he instructed them not to join groups that threatened

REMEMBERING WASHINGTON

The nation and the world mourned Washington's death, which occurred December 14, 1799. Congress voted to build a large marble monument in Washington's honor in the new capital.

Yet even in death, Washington sparked debate and division between the political parties. The Federalists favored a monument design featuring a grand pyramid. But the Democratic-Republicans disapproved because it resembled a tomb for a king. One Democratic-Republican proposed installing only a simple tablet to remember the president. When Democratic-Republicans gained the majority in Congress and Thomas Jefferson became president in 1801, interest in the monument faded. Construction did not begin until almost 50 years after Washington's death.

The Washington National Monument Society was formed to raise money to build a monument to honor the founding father that would be "unparalleled in the world." Robert Mills designed the monument in the style of an ancient Egyptian obelisk. The cornerstone was laid July 4, 1848. Construction stopped several times for financial and political reasons before its dedication in 1885. At the time it was the tallest structure in the world, standing just over 555 feet (169 meters) tall.

The Washington Monument in Washington, D.C., is one of many U.S. memorials to the first president.

the rights and happiness of others. Betraying his fear of political parties, he emphasized that the strength of the nation lay in its unity. Tenderly he suggested to the citizens to remember "the name of American, which belongs to you," and which should be a source of patriotism and pride.

Washington communicated his deep worry for the young nation finding its way among world powers. After risking his reputation to protect the United States from wars with European powers, Washington recommended simple relationships with other countries based only on trade. His firmest advice to the nation was to avoid permanent alliances with foreign countries.

George and Martha Washington set a precedent for how the president and spouse should receive guests.

By remaining self-reliant, the nation could avoid unnecessary war, or so he hoped.

The first president of the United States humbly described himself as "a servant of the public." But his stature in American history is far greater than if he had ruled as a king with absolute authority. By accepting the challenge of being a new kind of leader, of which the world provided no clear example, he essentially invented the office of the American president. Years after Washington's death, Thomas Jefferson himself credited the first American president with overseeing the "birth of a government, new in its forms and principles."

Beyond his accomplishments, Washington set a powerful precedent for all American presidents. Before taking office he wrote of doubting his "political skill" and put his faith firmly in the one quality he was certain he could bring to the presidency, his "integrity." During a difficult time in Washington's presidency, John Jay wrote of his happiness at having a president who considered "his own interest as inseparable from the public good." This selfless sense of duty explains why generations of Americans have considered Washington not merely a great leader, but the "father of our country."

TIMELINE

1732
George Washington is born February 22 in Westmoreland County, Virginia, to Augustine and Mary Washington

1753–1758
During the French and Indian War, Washington fights alongside British forces and later rises to commander of the Virginia militia

1775
Washington is elected delegate to the Second Continental Congress, appointed a general, and named commander in chief of the Continental army

1774
Washington is elected delegate to the First Continental Congress, where delegates discuss frustrations over British trade policies with the American colonies

1793
Washington is re-elected unanimously for a second term and issues the Neutrality Proclamation

1794
The Whiskey Rebellion breaks out in western Pennsylvania, and the Battle of Fallen Timbers marks the end of the Northwest Indian War

1789
Washington is unanimously elected first president of the United States and takes the oath of office in New York City

1759
Washington marries Martha Dandridge Custis, a wealthy widow from Virginia

1761
Washington inherits the estate Mount Vernon from his elder half-brother

1776
After several difficult losses, in December Washington launches a surprise attack on British forces at Trenton, New Jersey, reigniting hope in the Americans' cause

1783
With the British forces beaten, Washington resigns as commander in chief and retires to Mount Vernon

1795
Washington signs the controversial Jay Treaty to improve trade with Great Britain; American and Spanish negotiators resolve territory and trade disputes

1799
Washington dies of pneumonia at Mount Vernon on December 14

1796
Washington publishes his Farewell Address in a newspaper and retires to Mount Vernon

GLOSSARY

alliance—a favorable relationship between two countries

aristocracy—a society in which a small ruling class holds most of the power and often owns most of the land

bill—a written draft of a proposed law, which becomes official once leaders debate and approve it

confederation—a collection of people or groups that join together for a common cause

inauguration—a ceremony introducing a new leader to his or her citizens

militia—a small military group often used to keep order during emergencies

monarchy—a country ruled by a king or queen

oath—a formal promise to do a particular thing

republic—a country governed by representatives who are elected by the general population

treaty—an agreement between two or more countries

tyrant—a ruler who uses power in an unfair way

unanimous—something to which everyone agrees

unauthorized—not approved

veto—the ability of a leader to prevent something, such as a law, from taking effect

ADDITIONAL RESOURCES

FURTHER READING

Delano, Marfe Ferguson. *Master George's People: George Washington, His Slaves, and His Revolutionary Transformation.* Washington, D.C.: National Geographic, 2013.

Hollar, Sherman, ed. *George Washington.* New York: Britannica Educational Pub. with Rosen Educational Services, 2013.

Hubbard-Brown, Janet. *How the Constitution Was Created.* New York: Chelsea House Publishers, 2007.

INTERNET SITES

Use FactHound to find Internet sites related to this book. All of the sites on FactHound have been researched by our staff.

Here's all you do:

Visit *www.facthound.com*

Type in this code: 9780756549282

CRITICAL THINKING USING THE COMMON CORE

George Washington was reluctant to become president. What political and social challenges during his difficult second term could have influenced his refusing a third term? (Key Ideas and Details)

Throughout his presidency Washington's ideas and philosophies often reflected those of Alexander Hamilton and the Federalist Party. If Washington had been more influenced by Thomas Jefferson, how do you think he would have handled situations such as the Whiskey Rebellion or relations with Great Britain and France differently? What could have been the positive and negative consequences? (Integration of Knowledge and Ideas)

As the first American president, Washington set an example of how presidents should behave and make decisions. Which of his leadership qualities do you think earned him the affectionate term "father of our country"? Which personal qualities do you think also make him the admired leader he is today? (Key Ideas and Details)

SOURCE NOTES

Page 6, line 3: Ron Chernow. "George Washington: The Reluctant President." *Smithsonian Magazine*, Feb. 2011. 23 Feb. 2014. http://www.smithsonianmag.com/history-archaeology/George-Washington-The-Reluctant-President.html

Page 7, line 3: James Flexner. *George Washington and the New Nation (1783–1793)*. Boston: Little, Brown, 1970, p. 172.

Page 8, line 10: "George Washington: The Reluctant President."

Page 10, line 9: *George Washington and the New Nation (1783–1793)*, p. 187.

Page 11, line 1: "Washington's Inaugural Address of 1789." National Archives and Records Administration. 23 Feb. 2014. http://www.archives.gov/exhibits/american_originals/inaugtxt.html

Page 14, line 4: "From George Washington to Catharine Sawbridge Macaulay Graham, 9 January 1790." National Archives: Founders Online. 23 Feb. 2014. http://founders.archives.gov/documents/Washington/05-04-02-0363

Page 17, line 2: *George Washington and the New Nation (1783–1793)*, p. 420.

Page 17, line 3: "Washington's Inaugural Address of 1789."

Page 20, line 2: "George Washington to Edmund Randolph, September 28, 1789." American Memory: The George Washington Papers at the Library of Congress, 1741–1799. 23 Feb. 2014. http://memory.loc.gov/cgi-bin/query/r?ammem/mgw:@field(DOCID + @lit(gw300376))

Page 23, line 21: "From George Washington to David Humphreys, 16 Mar. 1791." National Archives: Founders Online. 23 Feb. 2014. http://founders.archives.gov/documents/Washington/05-07-02-0326

Page 26, line 1: *George Washington and the New Nation (1783–1793)*, p. 283.

Page 26, line 9: Thomas Jefferson. *The Writings of Thomas Jefferson*. Cambridge: Cambridge University Press, 2011, p. 168.

Page 31, line 3: "The Proclamation of Neutrality 1793." Yale Law School: The Avalon Project. 23 Feb. 2014. http://avalon.law.yale.edu/18th_century/neutra93.asp

Page 32, line 22: James Flexner. *George Washington: Anguish and Farewell (1793–1799)*. Boston: Little, Brown, 1972, p. 64.

Page 35, line 9: "From George Washington to Robert Morris, 12 Apr. 1786." National Archives: Founders Online. 23 Feb. 2014. http://founders.archives.gov/documents/Washington/04-04-02-0019

Page 37, line 15: *George Washington: Anguish and Farewell (1793–1799)*, p. 164.

Page 38, line 6: Ibid., p. 180.

Page 41, line 10: "From George Washington to the United States Senate, 16 Apr. 1794." National Archives: Founders Online. 23 Feb. 2014. http://founders.archives.gov/documents/Washington/05-15-02-0473

Page 46, line 8: "From George Washington to the Commissioners to the Southern Indians, 29 Aug. 1789." National Archives: Founders Online. 23 Feb. 2014. http://founders.archives.gov/documents/Washington/05-03-02-0326

Page 50, line 3: "George Washington." Bill of Rights Institute. 23 Feb. 2014. http://billofrightsinstitute.org/resources/educator-resources/founders/george-washington/

Page 51, line 5: Don Higginbotham. *George Washington Reconsidered*. Charlottesville: University Press of Virginia, 2001, p. 316.

Page 52, line 2: *George Washington: Anguish and Farewell (1793–1799)*, p. 271.

Page 52, line 6: Ibid., p. 272.

Page 52, line 8: "From George Washington to Thomas Jefferson, 23 Aug. 1792." National Archives: Founders Online. 23 Feb. 2014. http://founders.archives.gov/documents/Washington/05-11-02-0009

Page 53, line 4: "Farewell Address, September 17, 1796." American Memory: The George Washington Papers at the Library of Congress, 1741–1799. 23 Feb. 2014. http://memory.loc.gov/cgi-bin/ampage?collId = mgw2&fileName = gwpage024.db&recNum = 228

Page 53, sidebar, line 16: "Rediscovering George Washington: Farewell Address." PBS.org. 23 Feb. 2014. http://www.pbs.org/georgewashington/milestones/farewell_address_about.html

Page 53, sidebar, line 24: "February 22, 1862: Washington's Farewell Address." United States Senate: Senate Stories. 23 Feb. 2014. http://www.senate.gov/artandhistory/history/minute/Washingtons_Farewell_Address.htm

Page 54, line 15: "Washington Monument National Monument: History and Culture." National Park Service. 23 Feb. 2014. http://www.nps.gov/wamo/historyculture/index.htm

Page 55, line 3: "George Washington's Farewell Address, 1796." Bill of Rights Institute. 23 Feb. 2014. http://billofrightsinstitute.org/founding-documents/primary-source-documents/washingtons-farewell-address/

Page 56, line 4: *George Washington and the New Nation (1783–1793)*, p. 420.

Page 56, line 10: *George Washington: Anguish and Farewell (1793–1799)*, p. 502.

Page 56, line 14: *George Washington and the New Nation (1783–1793)*, p. 172.

Page 56, line 18: *George Washington: Anguish and Farewell (1793–1799)*, p. 28.

SELECT BIBLIOGRAPHY

"Bill of Rights." National Archives. http://www.archives.gov/exhibits/charters/bill_of_rights.html

Chernow, Ron. "George Washington: The Reluctant President." *Smithsonian Magazine.* Feb. 2011. http://www.smithsonianmag.com/history-archaeology/George-Washington-The-Reluctant-President.html

Cohen, Sheldon S. "Monuments to Greatness: George Dance, Charles Polhill, and Benjamin West's Design for a Memorial to George Washington." *Virginia Magazine of History and Biography,* vol. 99, no. 2, 1991, pp. 187–203.

"Farewell Address, September 17, 1796." American Memory: The George Washington Papers at the Library of Congress, 1741–1799. http://memory.loc.gov/cgi-bin/ampage?collId=mgw2&fileName=gwpage024.db&recNum=228

"First U.S. President Elected." History.com. http://www.history.com/this-day-in-history/first-us-president-elected

Flexner, James Thomas. *George Washington and the New Nation (1783–1793).* Boston: Little, Brown, 1970.

Flexner, James Thomas. *George Washington: Anguish and Farewell (1793–1799).* Boston: Little, Brown, 1972.

"George Washington, a National Treasure: The Portrait." National Portrait Gallery. http://www.georgewashington.si.edu/portrait/dress.html

"George Washington's Inaugural Address." National Archives and Records Administration. http://www.archives.gov/legislative/features/gw-inauguration/

"Gilder Lehram Collection Documents: Presidential Years." PBS: Rediscovering George Washington. http://www.pbs.org/georgewashington/father/index.html

"The Man Who Would Not Be King." Cato Institute. http://www.cato.org/publications/commentary/man-who-would-not-be-king

National Archives: Founders Online. http://founders.archives.gov/

"Native American Policy." George Washington's Mount Vernon. http://www.mountvernon.org/employees-navigation-level-1/encyclopedia-top-level/presidency/native-american-policy

"Slavery and Enslaved Community." George Washington's Mount Vernon. http://www.mountvernon.org/educational-resources/encyclopedia/slavery

Unger, Harlow Giles. *The Unexpected George Washington: His Private Life.* Hoboken, N.J.: John Wiley & Sons, 2006.

"Washington's Farewell Address." United States Senate: Art & History. http://www.senate.gov/artandhistory/history/minute/Washingtons_Farewell_Address.htm

INDEX

ABOUT THE AUTHOR

Danielle Smith-Llera has taught literature, writing, history, and visual arts to students ranging from elementary school to college. As the spouse of a diplomat, she has lived with her family in Washington, D.C., and New Delhi, India. They currently live in warm, green Kingston, Jamaica.